WHAT IS RED AND ROUND AND GOES PUTT-PUTT?
WHAT IS GRAY AND LUMPY AND COMES IN A CAN?
WHAT IS ROUND, HAS SEEDS AND GOES HONK-HONK?

Whether or not you know the answers to these riddles, Polly Cameron's latest book of nonsense will surprise you. Here is no ordinary collection of riddles, but a mad and merry world of humor. A world where elephants hide in cherry trees,

giraffes ride in Volkswagens, frogs have hand grenades and monkeys use ballpoint bananas. A world where everything is precisely what it should <u>not</u> be.

Brilliantly designed, each picture is Polly Cameron at her best and each page is an invention in itself —as ridiculous as the riddle it portrays.

WHAT <u>IS</u> RED AND ROUND AND GOES PUTT-PUTT? The answer will satisfy anyone young enough to laugh.

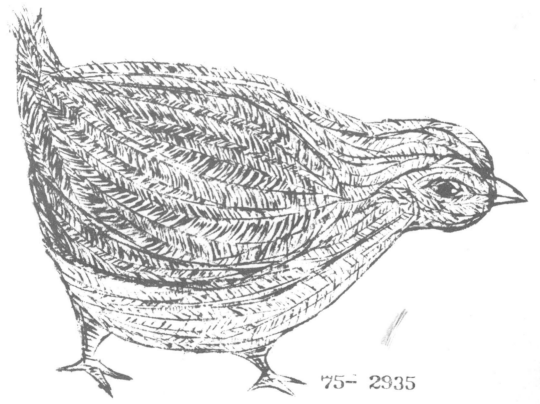

75- 2935

THE 2 TON CANARY
& OTHER NONSENSE RIDDLES
BY POLLY CAMERON

Coward, McCann & Geoghegan, Inc.   New York

Library of Congress Catalog Card Number: 65-20387

MANUFACTURED IN THE UNITED STATES OF AMERICA

Ninth Impression

PHOTOGRAPHY BY FRED BURRELL

THIS BOOK IS DEDICATED TO MY "EDITORS," CALLIE ANGEL AND ELIZABETH MILES.
THANK YOU FOR YOUR ASTUTE DIRECTION, CRITICISM AND INVALUABLE SUGGESTIONS.

My additional thanks to the following contributors:

Kim Agnew, Michael Brown, James Canfield, Chris Cooper, Laurie Coplin, Karen Eisenstat, Tom Farrell, Rick Fenton, Jamie Fouss, Rhona Free, Debby Gagliano, Denny Giffs, Sheryl Grabar, Gordon Gray, Pamela Gross, Geri Hammer, Mike Harris, Jana Johns, Ellen Kaufman, Sandra Kay, Sherry Koizim, Edward Kowalski, Edward Kramer, Mary Kramer, Liz Marks, Nan Marks, Peter Marks, Joe McPartland, Susan Mehlman, Helen Miles, Sara Miles, Ellen Miras, Jan Mittleman, Jill Olesker, Sidney Putz, Johnny Ratcliff, Teddy Ritter, Sandra Rosoff, Ceci Seaber, John Sestanovich, Martha Siegel, Debby Sinclair, Edgar Stewart, Charles Tate, Karen Thayer, David Trachtenberg, Kristan Walker, Kathy Wasserman, Sue Webster and Tom Webster

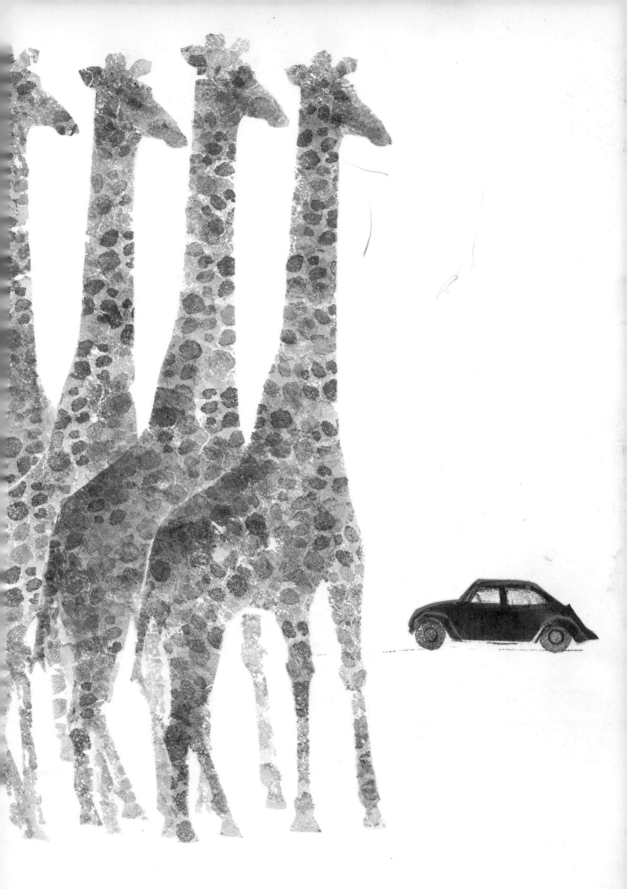

HOW DO YOU GET 4 GIRAFFES IN A VOLKSWAGEN?

2 IN FRONT, 2 IN BACK

WHAT'S RED AND GOES CLICK-CLICK?

A RED BALLPOINT BANANA

A RED WRINKLED ROCK WALKER

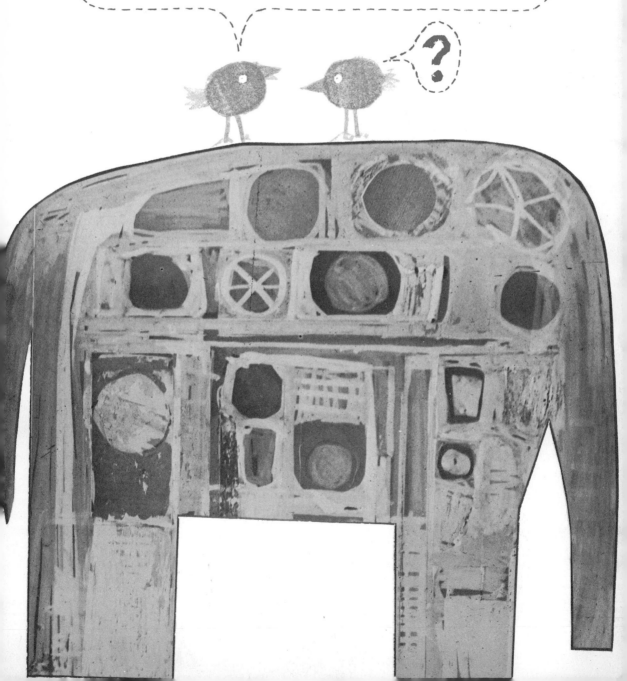

A MOUSE ON VACATION

A CROW WITH A MACHINE GUN

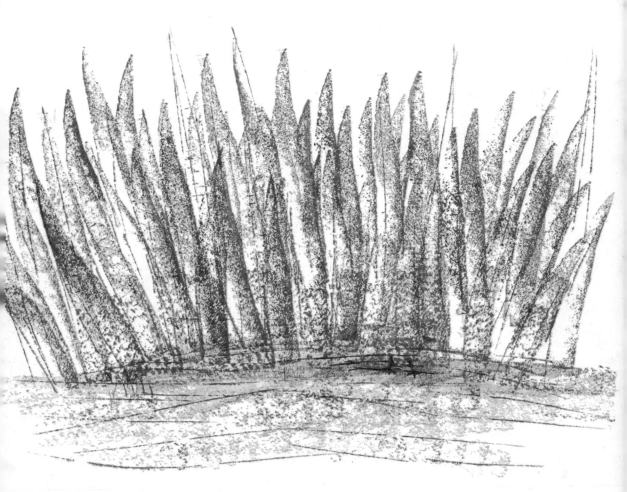

A FROG WITH A HAND GRENADE

WHEN DO ELEPHANTS WEAR RED SNEAKERS?

WHEN THEIR WHITE SNEAKERS ARE IN THE WASH

TO KEEP THEIR SNEAKERS DRY

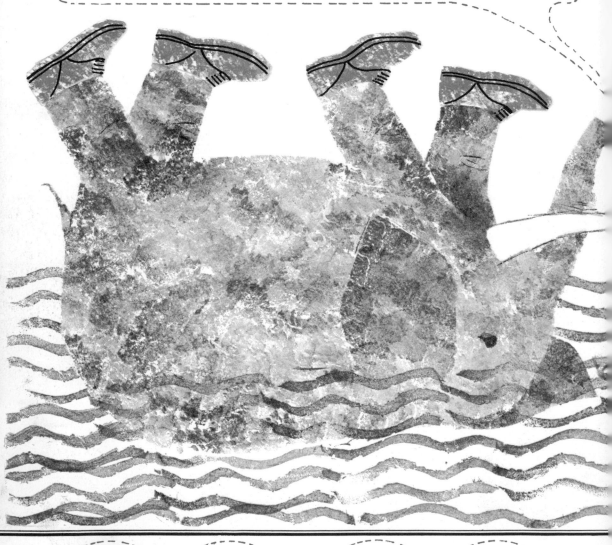

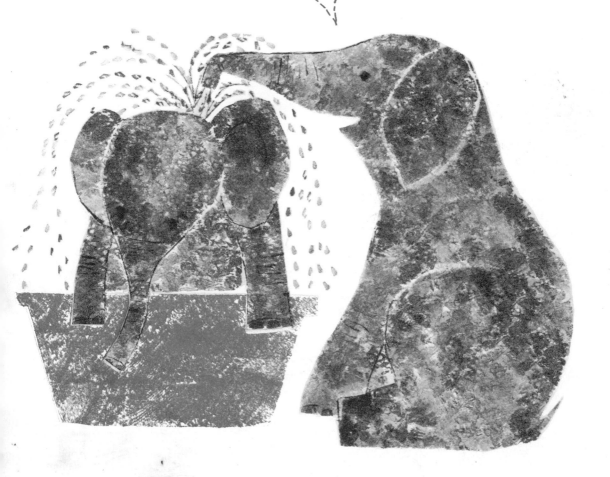

1 SCOOP OF ICE CREAM, 2 SQUIRTS OF SODA,
3 SCOOPS OF ELEPHANT

TO STAMP OUT FOREST FIRES

AN ELECTRIC RADISH

CREAM OF ELEPHANT SOUP

WHY ARE THERE SPOTS ON OCELOTS?

WHAT
DID THE
TWO-TON
CANARY
SAY
AS HE
PROWLED
DOWN
THE
DARK
ALLEY
AT
MIDNIGHT?

HERE KITTY KITTY

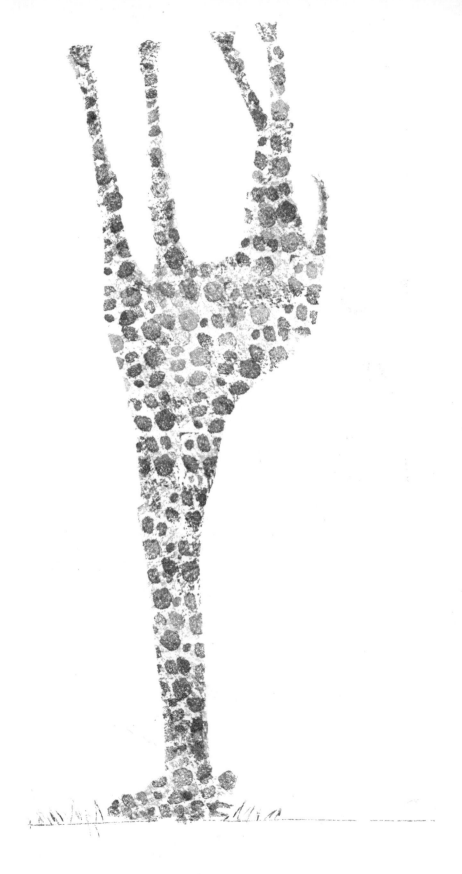

WHY DID THE GIRAFFE STAND ON HIS HEAD?

olly Cameron is an artist of varied talents. She
 the author and illustrator of seven books for
ildren, in addition to her work as a sculptor and
raphic designer.

lthough she has had no formal art training
which might account for her very original ap-
roach to design) she has worked in all areas of
raphic design during the past 15 years, inter-
upted only by a three-year-tour of Europe and
orth Africa. Her interests, like her talents, are
aried. Among them: "art and design of all kinds,
my classic Morgan sports car, my French sheep dog
and my home, a 150-year-old Victorian-Gothic
house overlooking the Hudson River in Sneden's
Landing, New York; to sum it up, all things which
are nice to look at and to be with."

Other books by Polly Cameron, *The Cat Who
Thought He Was a Tiger, The Cat Who Couldn't
Purr, The Dog Who Grew Too Much, The Boy
Who Drew Birds, A Child's Book of Nonsense*
and *"I Can't," Said the Ant.*